Original title:
Mossy Memories

Copyright © 2025 Creative Arts Management OÜ
All rights reserved.

Author: Julian Montgomery
ISBN HARDBACK: 978-1-80567-036-0
ISBN PAPERBACK: 978-1-80567-116-9

## **Echoes of a Hidden Past**

In the corner where shadows dance,
A shoe with laces, lost at a glance.
It whispers tales of my clumsy youth,
And of adventures that stretched the truth.

An old tin can, with secrets inside,
I caught a frog thinking it was a ride.
Jumps turned out to be quite the show,
Now a wet sock, an old tale I know.

## Green Haze of Yesterday

Beneath the layers of wilted leaf,
I found a gum wrapper, oh what a thief!
That sticky treasure—what a delight,
A memory sweet as in bright sunlight.

A tree house that once touched the sky,
Now a wobbly fort where squirrels comply.
With branches that creak and a bark that sighs,
The tales it tells could win a surprise.

## Fern Fronds and Faded Dreams


Among fronds that curl with rustic flair,
Lie stories of laughter, lost in the air.
There's a frog who thinks he's a royal king,
Croaking out ballads of an odd little fling.

A rubber band slingshot made to impress,
But aimed at my brother—oh what a mess!
He ducked in a hurry, his snack on the run,
As I burst out laughing—such chaotic fun!

## Tapestry of Time's Touch

Under layers of dust, a hat sits tight,
Once the crown of a knight, now a sorry sight.
It hid secrets of a wild, playful spree,
When pirates roamed freely, just wait and see!

A collection of rocks, each a new story,
Became pet rocks, basking in all their glory.
As time waves its wand and laughs at our glee,
We cherish the past, just you and me.

## Herbaceous Echoes

In the garden where giggles grow,
A snail had a party, moving slow.
Daisies wore hats, quite a sight,
As the ants danced around by moonlight.

Toadstools whispered jokes in the breeze,
While worms played checkers beneath the trees.
Laughter bubbled up like a brook,
Even the clovers joined in the nook.

## The Stillness of Green Thoughts

Under leaves, the grasshoppers sing,
While lazy bees nap, avoiding spring.
A frog croaks puns, just for the fun,
As daisies sway, caught in the run.

Moles peek out with cheeky grins,
Sharing tales of their wild spins.
In the cucumber patch, secrets lie,
Under the watchful gaze of the sky.

## Revisiting Nature's Embrace

In the thicket, where shadows play,
A rabbit tells stories of yesterday.
With each rustling leaf, a chuckle shared,
Nature's humor, always prepared.

Squirrels debate which acorn's best,
While the sunflowers stand tall in jest.
Butterflies flutter, gossip in flight,
Painting the garden with colors so bright.

## Beyond the Grassy Edge

At the edge of the field, a ruckus arrives,
Where the frogs jump joyfully, nature's jives.
A wise old owl hoots, 'What's the fuss?'
While crickets join in, generating a buzz.

The wind tells tales of the flowers' spree,
Tickling the daisies, as happy as can be.
Caterpillars waltz in their leafy sweep,
In this festival of joy, the earth takes a leap.

## A Gentle Recall of Place

Once I stumbled on a log,
Where a squirrel stole my snack.
It chattered loud, a little hog,
Scampered off, a fuzzy black.

Green stuff danced in sunlit beams,
I tried to catch it in my hand.
It slipped away, revealing dreams,
Of pranks that only trees had planned.

## Whispers of the Forest Floor

Beneath my feet, a soft surprise,
A carpet thick, it tickled toes.
In playful shade where shadows rise,
The whispers of the dirt arose.

A worm wiggled with such flair,
It waved like it was quite the star.
Such humor in this wild affair,
I laughed, feeling peculiar!

## **Lichen-Laden Thoughts**

There's a patch where green meets gray,
A canvas painted by the rain.
I pondered life just the other day,
As a slug slipped past, quite the mane.

It turned to me, oh what a sight!
With a grin, it went real slow.
I marveled at this sly delight,
And thought, "How peculiar you grow!"

## Echoes Beneath the Canopy

In the shade, the laughter blooms,
Where acorns drop like tiny bombs.
The forest sings in funny tunes,
While critters dance to nature's qualms.

A chipmunk winks, a fickle tease,
As if to say, "Just watch me go!"
I chuckled at these woodland pleas,
And joined the show with much gusto!

## In the Shade of Ancient Trees

Underneath the twisted limbs,
I found a squirrel with tiny hymns.
He wore a hat, quite chic and neat,
And danced around on nimble feet.

A wise old owl, he winked at me,
Eating snacks from a leafy tree.
With every flap, he'd share a laugh,
As if to say, 'You're not so daft!'

## Journey Through the Understory

Down in the thicket, bushes hide,
A rabbit hops with goofy pride.
With ears so large, he trips and slips,
And tumbles down with silly flips.

A raccoon cheers, he's quite the chap,
Brought snacks along for a picnic nap.
They toast with berries, oh what a feast,
In this wild world, they party the least!

## **Cradled by the Earth**

The soil whispers secrets old,
Of worms who dance, both brave and bold.
They twirl around in a muddy race,
With roots that giggle and sneak a chase.

A plucky beetle, dressed in stripes,
Claims he can outpace all the gripes.
He zips and zooms like he's on fire,
While telling tales that never tire.

**Echoes from the Past**

In the glen where shadows play,
Time tickles leaves in a playful way.
A ghost of laughter floats on by,
With echoes of songs from days gone dry.

Old stories told by toads at night,
Of jumping contests, quite a sight!
Each croak and ribbit, a punchline shared,
In nature's fun, none were spared.

## Interludes in Green Hues

Under the shade where laughter blooms,
The squirrels hold court with silly tunes.
A fog of green where giggles sprout,
What secrets does that mossy carpet shout?

Along the path where old folks stroll,
They trip on roots, lose track of their goal.
Nature chuckles as they weave and dart,
The trees all giggle, it's quite the art.

In shadows cast by dancing leaves,
A chorus of whispers, the humor weaves.
Then a bird dives down, a flamboyant dive,
Grabbing the snacks, does nature connive?

So join the merriment, laugh and play,
In fields of green, we find our way.
With each silly hop and joyous cheer,
The world is brighter, year after year.

## Beneath the Veil of Greenery

Beneath soft sheets of emerald hue,
A frog belts out his raucous cue.
In this realm, no worries abide,
Even the slugs take a fast-paced ride!

A picnic set on a plush green mat,
Where sandwiches vanish—like that! Just spat!
A voice calls out, "Where is my cake?"
The ants march off, that's all it takes!

In the cracks of bark, old tales reside,
Whispering secrets that they can't hide.
A gopher grins with a chuckle and wink,
As he nibbles on roots, puts folks to think!

With delicious banter, the leaves sway,
Jokes linger on till the end of the day.
So let's revel in this playful spree,
Beneath the canopy, where we can be free.

## Adorned with Earth's Gift

A dappled sun paints patches bright,
While critters scamper, what a delight!
Mushrooms pop, wear hats so grand,
They throw a party in their earthbound band.

The grass whispers jokes in a soft, sweet breeze,
It shakes with laughter, it aims to please.
In this garden, mischief reigns, oh my!
Where daisies gossip, and tulips sigh.

With twirling vines and a wiggly dance,
Worms groove along, given half the chance.
Blades of grass tease with endless jest,
Beneath this green, we find our rest.

So gather friends for a day of glee,
In a world adorned with nature's decree.
Let joy sprout forth, a delightful lift,
In this place of wonders, there's plenty of gift.

## Old Pathways and New Beginnings

Down the old trail, where laughter flows,
With quirky signs and whimsied prose.
The stones chuckle as we trip and roll,
Each stumble adds depth to the stroll.

Around the bend, the mushrooms grin,
Sporting outfits as bold as sin.
Nature's stage is set for the show,
With little critters in tow as they go.

The old paths echo with tales of yore,
Of misadventures and much, much more.
The laughter lingers, a cheeky tease,
As memories bloom in the soft green breeze.

So come along, bring zest and cheer,
In this vibrant world, there's nothing to fear.
New beginnings await on these roads we wander,
With chuckles aplenty, let's keep them yonder!

## Secrets of the Old Root

Beneath the bark, whispers grow,
Tales of squirrels with hats in tow.
They plot and scheme, in hide-and-seek,
Creating mischief each day of the week.

Rabbits gossip, they nibble and tease,
About the hedgehog that stole their cheese.
A raccoon party thrown late at night,
With acorn cups raised, oh what a sight!

Old roots chuckle, sharing their puns,
While violets smile as the laughter runs.
The forest is lively, a magical place,
With secrets buried in every space.

**Time Woven in Ferns**

Across the glade, the ferns love to dance,
With whimsical steps, they take their chance.
A dandelion struts like a tiny star,
While a bumblebee buzzes, not too far.

They argue over sun and shade,
Ferns claim victory in a leafy parade.
While crickets play their evening tune,
As shadows stretch in the light of the moon.

Time spins gently in this green ballet,
Where laughter echoed from yesterday.
A tapestry woven, each leaf a thread,
In the comedy of life, where no one's misled.

## Soft Footfalls on Forgotten Trails

Through the woods, the whispers call,
Of lost adventures, both big and small.
With every step, the stories unfold,
Of cheeky chipmunks and mischief bold.

A mushroom giggles under the shade,
While hedgehogs chase the laughter they've made.
A snail in sunglasses, moving so slow,
Says, 'I'm the star of this rowdy show!'

Nature's stage filled with playful glee,
Where even the leaves can dance with me.
Old paths echo with smiles and cheer,
As frolicsome critters gather near.

# The Embrace of Ancient Earth

In the earth's embrace, a tickle awaits,
As critters hide behind soft green gates.
A root in the ground tells jokes with great flair,
While ants march in line, without a care.

The wise old stones, they chuckle and grin,
Blackberries tease the squirrels to spin.
A playful breeze whispers secrets of fun,
As sunbeams race the shadows they run.

In the cozy grasp of this timeless floor,
Each giggle blooms, rich stories in store.
From acorn cap to feathered flight,
The earth chuckles softly into the night.

# Reclamation by Nature

In the corner of the yard, a rubber duck,
Is now a pot for weeds, quite out of luck.
The garden gnomes have turned to outdoor jest,
Wearing mossy hats, they think they're the best.

A squirrel steals my snacks with cheeky flair,
While the old swing creaks, caught in mid-air.
I swear the daisies wink, a giggly spree,
As I try to rap with bees about my tea.

The sun wipes laughter off the lawn chair seat,
While daisies dance to the ants' busking beat.
Nature's reclaiming all that we've forgot,
With every chuckle from a mossy spot.

Each tree stands proud, with tales of old,
Of picnics, spills, and stories bold.
In the whispers of leaves, I hear a jest,
As I remember my wild backyard quest.

## Beneath the Canopy of Memory

Beneath the branches, a shadow plays,
With the laughter of kids from long-lost days.
The treehouse rocks like a ship in a storm,
Where squirrels salute and all ideas form.

Leaves gossip about the ice cream parade,
And how the popsicle made a grand escape.
An acorn drops, like confetti it falls,
A victory dance in the midst of it all.

The turtles laugh as they watch the race,
While I gingerly glance at my nonchalant face.
A picnic blanket, a pizza box shrine,
And ants marching by in perfect straight line.

Under the canopy, tales twist and bend,
Where giggles and whispers, they never end.
And if the grass is plush, like a living rug,
I'll dive right in and give a big hug.

## **Where Time Slows in Green**

In a blanket of grass, time takes a break,
A ladybug smiles, for goodness' sake.
The old tricycle rusts, a throne in disguise,
While butterflies debate the best kind of pie.

As frogs play chess on the pond's glassy face,
A slow turtle wanders at a leisurely pace.
The weeds throw a party, quite uninvited,
As my shoe gets stuck, and I feel slighted.

Laughter rings out from the faded swing,
And crickets join in, making the night sing.
A breeze whispers secrets of candy and fun,
As I reminisce about each sparkling pun.

The oak stands tall, a guardian grand,
Holding the memories of this funny land.
In the heart of the green, with joy I lean,
Where the world slows down and is forever seen.

## Dreams Woven in Bittersweet Shade

Under the arch of the willow's embrace,
The breeze tells stories, a delightful chase.
My dreams float by like balloons on a string,
Each one a giggle, oh, what joy they bring.

The grass tickles toes that dare to roam,
While shadows weave laughter, so far from home.
A rubber band battle with socks in the air,
As I dodge the daisies, living without care.

A picnic basket bursts with laughs and spills,
And lemonade rivers run down winding hills.
The twilight giggles at the moon's silly grin,
As fireflies join in for a bright, buzzing din.

In the shade of the trees, time learns to dance,
And every small moment gets a fresh chance.
Life's a funny riddle, a whimsical trade,
We find joy in the laughter that nature just made.

## **Sunkissed Shadows on Cool Stone**

Under the sun, the shadows play,
Dancing around in a quirky way.
The stones chuckle, feeling bright,
Whispering secrets in the light.

Lizards lounge with a flair of swag,
On paths where giggles and chuckles snag.
Butterflies flit with a wink and a spin,
As if they know where the fun begins.

On a picnic blanket, ants march in line,
Carrying crumbs, like it's divine.
Squirrels drop acorns with style and panache,
Creating a ruckus, a lighthearted clash.

The stones are the audience, giggling in glee,
As laughter echoes beneath the tree.
In every crevice, joy does reside,
A playground of memories where fun won't hide.

## Remnants of Gentle Breezes

In a field where old weeds sway,
The breeze brings forth a funny ballet.
A tumbleweed rolls with a cheeky grin,
While daisies giggle at where they've been.

The sunbeams wink through the leaves so green,
Tickling the flowers, ruled by the unseen.
A dandelion's puff makes a bold flight,
While the chubby bumblebee zips left and right.

Fluttering leaves burst into cheers,
Laughing at nothing, just tickling ears.
When the breeze blows, it's quite the show,
A whimsical dance with a twirl and a flow.

Even the clouds join the playful spree,
Making shapes that giggle with glee.
In the soft whispers of wind's sweet tickle,
Memories bloom in laughter's quick fickle.

## Where the Pines Hold Secrets

Under tall pines, a squirrel awaits,
Stashing acorns and filling his plates.
He listens closely; here's the scoop,
Whispers of critters create a fun troop.

Branches sway as if sharing a tale,
Of adventures where laughter prevails.
The pines are guardians, with chuckles old,
Guarding the joy that never gets cold.

The forest floor is home to the jest,
Where mushrooms giggle in their tiny vest.
A fox struts by, with a wink and a grin,
Wearing the mischief; oh, where to begin?

In a nook, a chipmunk holds court,
Telling his tales in a comical short.
The pines, they giggle, swaying with pride,
For where there's laughter, the world gets wide.

## **Beneath Layers of Time**

Beneath the rock, where the shadows sleep,
Funny little memories begin to creep.
Dusty old corners hold laughter so sweet,
With echoes of kids racing on their feet.

The passageways twist like a riddle untold,
Where the past meets the present, brave and bold.
A moth flits by with a tuxedo flair,
While old cobwebs laugh without a care.

In secret layers, the giggles arise,
As time takes a break, and fun never dies.
Wrinkles and crevices show their delight,
As memories dance in the soft evening light.

Here, laughter is stitched in crumbling seams,
Woven together in joyful dreams.
Each step reveals a faint, funny chime,
Echoes of joy beneath layers of time.

## Fragments of Sentiment

In the garden where laughter grew,
A gnome in a hat, bright and blue.
He whispered secrets, oh so sly,
While bees danced by and clouds floated high.

A squirrel once tried to join the chat,
With acorn hat and a fancy spat.
But he tripped on roots, oh what a sight!
We laughed so hard, it felt just right.

## Repose Amongst Nature's Lushness

A hammock hung between two trees,
Where I napped and heard the breeze.
A raccoon peeked with a cheeky grin,
'Can I join you?' he asked, 'I'll bring a sin!'

He brought some snacks and spilled a drink,
While I just chuckled, needing to think.
We shared a feast, it was quite absurd,
As squirrels cheered, and laughter stirred.

## Unraveling Amongst the Ferns

Ferns danced lightly in the sun,
A ribboned path that promised fun.
I lost my shoe in a patch of green,
'This is the worst!' I laughed, 'What a scene!'

The frogs croaked laughter, joining in,
As I hopped on one foot with a goofy grin.
A nearby snail gave a slow applause,
'You're on a roll, just without the pause!'

## The Silent Song of Yesteryears

Old photos hide in a dusty box,
A dog wearing shades, a turtle in socks.
I chuckled hard at those silly days,
When all we needed were wild forest plays.

We'd race the wind, just kids with dreams,
Under the guise of sunlight beams.
And though those days can't come again,
I'll treasure them all with my silly grin.

## Melodies of the Hidden Grove

In the woods where whispers play,
Squirrels hold a concert day.
With acorn drums, they tap away,
While rabbits dance in bright array.

A frog croaks out a silly tune,
The trees sway under the noon.
Owls spin tales of a raccoon,
Who wears a hat and sings to the moon.

The breeze carries a laughter light,
As fireflies join in the night.
With every flutter, pure delight,
These woodland spirits feel so bright.

Beneath the boughs where shadows play,
The stories twist in a funny way.
In hidden nooks, the echoes stay,
A symphony of joy on par with clay.

# Revisited in the Green

A patch of grass, a dreamer's throne,
A gnome grins wide, he's never alone.
With mushrooms dressed in hats and scone,
   They sip on tea made from pinecone.

The bees wear shades, so cool and neat,
   While butterflies dance to the beat.
   A ladybug's quite the elite,
   She twirls about with tiny feet.

A hammock swings with a gentle creak,
While chipmunks scheme in a game of peek.
   Tales of the past they lovingly tweak,
   Bringing smiles with every cheek.

And there it hums, the laughter ring,
   As nature's crowd starts to sing.
   In every leaf, a giggle's fling,
   A melody that makes hearts spring.

## **Cradles of Forgotten Stories**

Beneath the bramble, tales ensue,
Of hedgehogs who brewed a tasty stew.
They laughed so loud, the sky turned blue,
In cradles of tales that grew and grew.

The shadows dance, a tickle-fight,
As fireflies join in with delight.
An owl insists it's all polite,
To share a snack under moonlight.

With whispers of the days gone past,
The woodland jokes are sure to last.
A wily fox scurries by fast,
Saying, "What fun! Let's have a blast!"

In every nook where laughter roams,
Are echoes playing with wooden homes.
The secrets shared like drifting foams,
Bring joy to those returning gnomes.

## Nature's Time Capsule

A riddle lives inside each stone,
Where rabbits gossip and seeds are sown.
With silly faces, they have grown,
In nature's keepsake, joys are flown.

A babbling brook sings in a jest,
Where fish wear crowns and never rest.
The trees engage in a game of chess,
With squirrels playing for the best.

The sunbeams sprinkle glitter trails,
As ants hold parades with their tiny flails.
A butterfly giggles, and never pales,
While spinning yarns of grand details.

In every rustle, every sound,
The joy of earth can easily be found.
From roots to skies, in laughter bound,
Nature's time holds wonders profound.

## The Dance of the Dappled Light

In the forest where shadows play,
Bouncing beams lead the way.
Squirrels prance in and out,
While the birds just laugh and shout.

Leaves twist in a sunlit jig,
Mice stomp with a tiny gig.
They spin and twirl with glee,
As if the world's a grand marquee.

Glimmers peek through the trees,
Who knew green could feel so free?
The sun's a spotlight for the show,
Every creature dressed to glow.

When twilight fades the dance does wane,
Yet the echoes still remain.
The light may dim, but the fun,
Is forever a forest run.

## Glistening Ghosts of the Past

Through the mist, where whispers creep,
Old echoes that make me leap.
A frog croaks tribute to the night,
Its laughter causes quite a fright.

Once a tree, now a clumsy stump,
Wobbling as if to thump.
Feeling spry, yet oh-so-slow,
Who knew wood could put on a show?

Fungi dance and giggle with glee,
Haunting tales of days carefree.
The breeze carries with it a jest,
An invitation to their fest.

In the shadows of yesteryear,
They beckon with crooked cheer.
Unruly memories laugh and play,
As the night wiggles away.

## **Ribbons of Green in Twilight**

Frogs in ties of leafy green,
Spin tales of things unseen.
Slippery paths twist and curl,
As critters join in the whirl.

Vines drape low like frilly skirts,
While fireflies flirt in flirts.
The ground chuckles, mosses sway,
Beneath a sky that turns to gray.

Sneaky toads hop in a line,
Making mischief, feeling fine.
Critters court, the night is light,
As laughter dances, pure delight.

In the fading, softest glow,
Giggles spill where few will go.
So come and join this froggy feast,
As the twilight teases—never ceased.

## A Symphony of Soft Growth

In a glade where giggles sprout,
Nature's chorus sings no doubt.
Sprigs of green with secrets grow,
And the shy buds whisper low.

Dandelions burst into song,
With a dance that's bouncy and long.
They tickle the air, so spry and bold,
While butterflies start to unfold.

Each mossy patch a seat for fun,
Where beetles boast and critters run.
A banter sweet, as laughter flows,
Through the tangled tales of rows.

Early morn, an orchestra plays,
Nature's symphony, wild displays.
A tickling breeze, a jostling jest,
In the green, we find our rest.

## Retrospective Under the Boughs

Under the boughs where we used to roam,
Frogs serenaded us like we were home.
I slipped on a log, took a dive with a grin,
Landed in mud, thought I'd never win.

We'd race the clouds, oh what a sight!
Trying to catch bugs that took to flight.
Laughter echoed through thick green air,
Memories sprouted, our wild little lair.

We'd climb every tree like we knew no bounds,
Pretending we ruled those enchanted grounds.
With every stumble, we'd burst out in glee,
Who knew mischief could feel so free?

So here's to revisiting times that were bright,
To chaos and giggles, all pure delight.
May the laughter continue, let's not be shy,
For memories, like pets, are never goodbye!

## The Resilient Palette of Time

Colors of childhood, splashed wide and bold,
Crayons in hand, our stories unfold.
With each little doodle, a giggle ignites,
As we drew up our worlds, full of fanciful sights.

Oh, how I painted the sun with a frown,
Rainbow emotions flopped upside down.
Finger-paint fight! A hue-tastic mess,
We laughed 'til we cried, felt so truly blessed.

With grass stains on knees, and cake on our shirts,
Each scuffle a canvas, we danced through the dirt.
The palette of joy, a riotous scene,
Who knew growing up could be this serene?

Time's kind paintbrush, gentle and warm,
Swirls of the past, in delight they form.
Let's raise a toast to our splashy delight,
In laughter, we'll sparkle, in memory, ignite!

## Secrets in the Soft Ground

In the soft ground slept treasures we found,
Dirt-clad secrets with giggles abound.
From trinkets to treasures, our spoils on display,
The neighborhood's pride, or so we would say.

Oh, the worms we misnamed, oh what a hoot,
Wiggly friends in this earthquaked loot.
We'd summon them forth, with dramatics so grand,
To parade all our critters, a wiggly band.

Our laughter would echo like old rusty springs,
As grasshoppers joined in on our fantasy flings.
What secrets we held in our tiny, bold hands,
Building grand castles, making curious plans.

So here's to the dirt, our throne and our stage,
Each giggle a chapter that we now engage.
May we treasure those secrets, forever abide,
In the soft ground of youth, let our joy hide.

## **Treading Through the Past**

Stepping through puddles of all that was done,
Splashing in mischief, oh what foolish fun!
Each caper a story that dances with cheer,
As footprints of laughter draw us ever near.

We'd tiptoe on grass, like spies on a quest,
Sneaking cookies, putting our skills to the test.
The kitchen our hideout, our safest retreat,
Where giggles and crumbs would sip on sweets.

With bicycles racing, we tore through the breeze,
Chasing down sunsets with so much ease.
Our memories flutter like leaves in the wind,
In the joyful parade that will never rescind.

So tread with a grin, let the past be our guide,
In laughter's embrace, we shall ever abide.
For each silly trip, and each playful jest,
Are echoes of joy that we cherish the best.

## Shadows in the Underbrush

A squirrel stole my sandwich, oh dear,
He darted away with no sign of fear,
In the shadows, he giggled, what a tease,
As I chased him around, stumbling with ease.

The raccoon joined in, what a pair,
He pointed and laughed, ate without a care,
With each misstep, they danced in delight,
Nature's comedy show, a laugh every night.

With twigs on my head, I slouched down low,
Hiding in tall grass, putting on a show,
While creatures passed by with their silly quips,
I'm just the punchline, as laughter sips.

But as the sun set, their joy took flight,
The critters grew weary, ending their night,
I waved goodbye to my furry old friends,
Until tomorrow, when the fun never ends!

## Hushed Reflections of Nature

A pond sat quietly, with frogs that croaked,
Each ribbit echoed 'til everyone choked,
The dragonflies giggled, all in a row,
While ducks quacked their peppy, punchy show.

A turtle, quite lazy, did stretch and yawn,
With each slow movement, he teased dawn,
The fish below splashed, a watery mess,
As the heron squawked, "I'm the one who's blessed!"

With shadows that whispered of silly old jokes,
The trees, they swayed, as if telling hoaxes,
A raccoon in the reeds, looking so spry,
Waved me goodbye with a twinkle in his eye.

The sun finally set, as stories ran dry,
Yet laughter lingered under the sky,
In the still of the evening, nature's delight,
With memories filed, I bid them goodnight.

## Softened Imprints of Time

In the garden where giggles softly reside,
Curly leaves whisper antics, a safe place to hide,
The ants play parade, with crumbs for a feast,\nWhile a ladybug lounges, brushing off yeast.

The carrots are laughing, all sprouted by chance,
As the tomatoes wiggled, refusing to dance,
With a raccoon tuxedo, they stood tall and true,
Making fun of the turnips, and all their hue.

As the sun set low, and shadows grew tall,
The dirt on my knees gave a nostalgic call,
With each tiny treasure unearthed in haste,
I gathered their charm, with no time to waste.

Yet laughter was cradled in every small patch,
Each seed sown, giggled in a sweet little catch,
As the garden grew quiet, the fun in repose,
In the softening dusk, the humor still glows.

## Verdant Secrets in the Shade

Beneath the big oak, the kids tried to hide,
In a fort built of leaves, where laughter can't bide,
Invasions from squirrels, they plotted their schemes,
While tossing acorns, igniting their dreams.

"Watch out!" one yelled, "the boogeyman's near!"
The laughter erupted; it echoed our cheer,
With shadows as allies, they leapt to the fray,
Fighting off monsters with giggles and play.

The sunlight filtered through branches so grand,
Each playful whisper, like grains of fine sand,
As grasshoppers danced, they joined in the fun,
While the sun peeked through, signaling their run.

As the day dissolved into twilight's soft haze,
The children adjourned to the night's cozy ways,
With secrets held tight, in the shade they had made,
Their laughter remains, in the memories they laid.

## Threads of Green in Remembrance

In a forest where time seems to pause,
Laughter echoes with nature's applause.
Fungi in hats dance on a log,
While squirrels plot mischief like an old frog.

Old trees whisper secrets in a breeze,
Tickling the branches, even the leaves tease.
We find lost socks in the roots so deep,
Wondering how they ever fell asleep!

Beneath bright sunlight, we peek and pry,
Searching for treasures in the green nearby.
A turtle in shades grimaces in glee,
As we trip over roots, oh, look at me!

With every turn and twist we take,
Life's little quirks make the laughter quake.
So, let's chase shadows and giggles galore,
In threads of green, we'll forever explore.

# Beneath the Soft Embrace

Beneath the trees, a carpet of green,
Where squirrels race as if unseen.
A raccoon giggles at our silly falls,
As we stumble and trip over mossy walls.

We build our forts in a patchy glade,
With branches and leaves, a whimsical parade.
Yet, dodging ants that march in a line,
Has us squealing like kids, feeling just fine!

Frogs croak a tune, all out of key,
Their musical charm, oh, so carefree.
We roll in the grass, as warm sun beams,
Chasing each other, lost in our dreams.

With laughter that echoes through shady bows,
Nature's warm hug is where humor grows.
Beneath the soft embrace, the world feels right,
As we share silly stories till the night!

## Secrets of the Woodland Floor

The woodland floor, a mystic site,
Where critters meet for a chat at night.
The chipmunks trade tales with a wry little grin,
While moss giggles softly, letting jokes in.

We find acorns that look quite a lot,
Like tiny hats that nature forgot.
As bunnies hop over, we shout with delight,
Dressing up pine cones, oh, what a sight!

Tumbling through leaves, we play hide and seek,
While caterpillars waltz, oh so sleek.
In this playful realm where giggles unite,
The secrets of joy shine unbelievably bright.

Every squishy patch holds quirky lore,
Where laughter can sprout like never before.
In shades of green, we roam and we sing,
In the heart of the woods, happiness springs.

## Tapestry of Time and Green

Amidst tangled roots and dewdrops' sheen,
We weave together a memory scene.
With each step forward, we stumble anew,
As vines seem to giggle, and branches ask, "Who?"

Squirrels in capes act as our guides,
While shadows play tricks where fun resides.
A dance on the path made of whispers and leaves,
As the world around us dances and weaves.

With every rustle, a story unfolds,
Of ancient trees and mischief that molds.
In laughter we find what nature bestows,
A tapestry bright where curiosity grows.

So let's frolic along this green thread of fun,
With smiles and surprises that weigh a ton.
In this playful realm that feels like a dream,
We'll cherish the laughter and let out a scream!

## The Soft Hymn of the Forest


In the woods where squirrels play,
I tripped on roots in a funny way.
A raccoon laughed and took a bow,
Saying, "Hey there, friend! You look quite wow!"

Leaves were dancing, mocking me,
Telling tales of clumsy glee.
I swear I saw a tree wink,
And I couldn't help but stop and think.

Now every time I hike that path,
I chuckle at my silly math.
For every step I take with grace,
A butterfly then takes my place.

So here I go, another try,
To bond with nature, oh me, oh my!
Yet all around, the trees just grin,
Reminding me where I've been.

## Traces of Yesterday

Once I found a crooked stick,
Thought it was a magic trick.
A gnome popped out with a tiny hat,
Said, "Put that down, you silly brat!"

I once climbed high to touch the sky,
And knocked my lunch down with a sigh.
The ants held a feast, in pure delight,
Dancing round the crumbs all night.

Old trees whisper tales of yore,
Their bark is full of legends galore.
I laughed so hard I nearly fell,
When one claimed he knew me well!

Each step back brings such sweet cheer,
Memories wrapped in nature's sphere.
With laughter echoing all around,
I embrace what joy I've found.

## **Time's Resilient Quilt**

Underneath the patchwork leaves,
I found some socks, oh how it weaves!
A squirrel giggled, said, "They're mine!"
I laughed and winked, but that's just fine.

The forest wears a quilt of fun,
Stitched together, each thread a pun.
With every step, I shuffle and sway,
While shadows dance to a silly ballet.

Colors burst in an odd display,
As birds join in the choir today.
They squawk and chirp with no subtlety,
And I join their chorus, oh so free!

Time rolls on, yet laughter stays,
Each woven moment sings and plays.
In this vibrant, tangled spree,
I find the bliss of being me.

## Upon the Softened Ground

Upon the ground where soft things grow,
Bounced a bunny, putting on a show.
It did a flip, then took a bow,
I laughed so hard, I lost my cow!

The earth is like a trampoline,
Bouncing dreams that feel so keen.
I landed near a wrinkled sage,
Who chuckled loud, "You're quite the page!"

With mushrooms wearing little hats,
And ladybugs engaged in chats,
The forest floor will always tease,
And make me giggle with such ease.

So every step I take around,
I find more joy upon this ground.
With every laugh, I grow more wise,
In nature's quirks, laughter lies!

## Green Shadows of Longing

In the garden, I lost my shoe,
Only to find a sneaky gnu.
He wears it with such panache,
Swishing away in a grassy dash.

With laughter hidden beneath each leaf,
I ponder my life's absurd beliefs.
Was it the gnu or my lost things?
A riddle wrapped in greenish flings?

Sneezing dandelions bloom in cheer,
As frogs croak tales we reluctantly hear.
Who knew shadows could dance and play?
With quirky friends, I'd choose to stay!

In this realm where shadows twirl,
Each misplaced item starts to whirl.
With giggles of grass and a gnu's proud walk,
Memory made of the laughter we'll mock.

## Beneath the Silent Boughs

Beneath branches so grand and old,
Squirrels chat secrets never told.
A nutty debate without a doubt,
As they chirp about who's the best scout.

Underneath a blanket of green,
A raccoon sneaks out for the unseen.
His bandit mask, oh what a sight,
Stealing snacks in the soft moonlight.

It's a comedy show each day anew,
With nature's misfits in every view.
Captured in the lenses of a bug-eyed beetle,
Life here is truly a wild teaser!

Among the laughs, we often think,
What if trees could actually blink?
A winking wink and a rustling cheer,
Whispers of joy are all we hear.

## Whispers of Life's Embrace

In the bramble, a breeze does sway,
Tickling noses in a playful way.
Buzzing bees hum a catchy tune,
While ants practice their best saloon.

With petals that giggle as they bloom,
Flowers dance in a colorful room.
Who knew a bee could hold a show?
With tricks that steal hearts; they steal the glow.

The meandering paths where moss resides,
Are filled with creatures playing hide and slide.
An earthworm winks, gives a little squirm,
Inviting you to join the squishy term.

To frolic in the laughter of creation,
Is to embrace life's wild celebration.
In nature's arms, so soft, so sweet,
Every tangle feels like a fun cheat.

## Enfolded in Nature's Grasp

In the forest's hug, so tight and warm,
Chipmunks plot their next grand charm.
They trade jokes with the swirling breeze,
While wishing on falling leaves with ease.

Stumbling over roots and rocks galore,
Who knew the forest could offer more?
A chorus of laughter echoes through,
As twigs tease toes, oh what a crew!

Amongst the laughter, a wise old tree,
Chuckles softly at the antics, you see.
With bark-lined wisdom and leaves aflutter,
He holds secrets like peanut butter.

So wander forth, where giggles play,
In nature's grasp, find joy each day.
With silly antics and playful sights,
Life unfurls in delightful bites.

## Recollections in Green

In the garden of my past,
There's a squirrel wearing a hat.
He once danced on a trash can lid,
Leaving all the neighbors flat.

The daisies giggle in a breeze,
Their petals play like tiny kites.
While a snail plays the saxophone,
To the rhythm of tree frogs' nights.

A shoe lost under the old oak,
Tells tales as old roots intertwine.
Two ants toss crumbs like confetti,
Deciding who's drinking the wine.

And when I wander through that place,
Life's a circus half the time.
Each moment blooms in vibrant hues,
With awkward joys, a silly rhyme.

## Fern Fronds and Forgotten Days

Beneath the ferns, a gnome snores loud,
Dreaming of a cat in a shroud.
He juggles acorns, quite the sight,
As crickets chirp their own delight.

In the shadows, a raccoon waits,
With a stash of sweet candy plates.
Laughing at the old turtle slow,
Who forgot where he's supposed to go.

A ladybug's dancing on a twig,
While beetles play a tiny gig.
They roll the dice on fallen leaves,
Designing rules that none believes.

Oh, the shadows recall blunders,
Of young hearts chasing flighty wonders.
A grand parade of silly dreams,
Where laughter flows like bubbling streams.

## The Life Beneath the Stones

Under stones, the creatures plot,
A game of hide and seek, why not?
A mole puts on a fancy shoe,
Declaring he's the best, it's true.

The slugs host parties, oh so bright,
With glittering shells in the night.
They tell tall tales of what they've seen,
As the toads croak out a scene.

A worm recites a love-haiku,
For an earthworm date with quite the view.
Fashioned in soil, they twirl and hug,
Embracing life's strange, squishy snug.

This realm is awkward but so grand,
Where ups and downs go hand in hand.
For even rocks can laugh and play,
In a world that's far from gray.

**Crumbled Leaves**

Crumbling leaves like old jokes fall,
As squirrels engage in a food brawl.
One pretends to be a chef, you see,
Mixing acorns with glee and glee!

The wind whispers, tickling their tails,
While crickets practice their weird scales.
A chipmunk sketches a plan to win,
Drawn in circles, with a cheeky grin.

Scattered whispers of past pursuits,
Festivities between little roots.
A pumpkin pie for the woodland crew,
Made from secrets and froggy stew.

A riddle hangs from a crooked branch,
As shadows sway in a wooden dance.
No one's serious, all in fun,
In the laughter that's never done.

## Gentle Dreams

In a world of winks and tiny beams,
Each creature shares its gentle dreams.
A squirrel dreams he can fly so high,
On fluffy clouds, he'll touch the sky.

The owls debate who's got the charm,
In moonlit meetings that disarm.
They toast to gossip of the day,
And quirkily dance till the sun's ray.

A worm daydreams of a fancy hat,
Worn by a chubby cheeky cat.
While frogs compose a ribbiting tune,
To serenade the sleeping moon.

Oh, how whimsy paints the light,
In soft giggles cloaked by night.
With hearts so full, they weave a seam,
Of joyous tales and gentle dreams.

## Whispers of the Forest Floor

In the woods where critters play,
I found a shoe, oh what a day!
It must belong to someone fast,
Who raced for fun but fell at last.

A squirrel chuckles, high in the trees,
While chatting to a band of bees.
They laugh at shoes and trips and slips,
Each giggle adds to nature's quips.

Remember when we tripped on roots?
Our laughter echoed, what a hoot!
The forest floor, a stage for fails,
With secret tales in every trail.

So here we stand, forever bright,
With mossy tales to share at night.
In every step where laughter starts,
Found treasures bloom in forest hearts.

## Echoes in the Green

Among the trees, the echoes ring,
As critters dance, and chipmunks swing.
A picnic planned with cake in hand,
   Until I tripped and fell on land.

The ants all cheered, raised tiny flags,
   As I surrendered all my swag.
"A feast for us!" the bushes squealed,
While I just flopped, a humor shield.

The trees share tales of silly sights,
Of raccoons stealing food at nights.
A dance beneath the moonlit beams,
Where laughter wakes our sweetest dreams.

So chase the trails and don't be shy,
Let giggles echo, reach the sky.
In leafy arms, let joy be keen,
As fun resides in shades of green.

## **Lichen-Laced Reminiscence**

Upon a rock, I rest my chin,
And think of all the goofy spins.
The world is bright with every hue,
Except the time I tripped on glue.

The waterfall laughed, it splashed so loud,
As mushrooms giggled in a crowd.
Not one was safe from nature's jest,
Each stumble felt like nature's test.

With laughter lurking all around,
In every crevice, joy is found.
Among the leaves, old stories flare,
Of silly falls and friendly bear.

Together we'll make memories bright,
In every nook, in every sight.
With laughter laced like vines of cheer,
In vibrant greens, we have no fear.

## Shadows Beneath the Canopy

Underneath the leafy dome,
We stumbled, lost, yet felt at home.
The shadows danced with a playful tease,
As branches swayed like mischievous bees.

A raccoon winked, with snacks in tow,
While we debated which way to go.
Each path we took led to a jest,
With every turn, a little test.

The whispers told of playful tricks,
Of further walks and hidden kicks.
In shadowy realms where laughter fell,
Nature weaved its joke so well.

So in the woods where shadows play,
Let's gather up those silly days.
With every step, let laughter flow,
In the heart of the woods, let joy just grow.

# Nature's Embracing Arms

In the forest, I often tread,
Where squirrels dance and laugh instead.
A twig snaps loud, I jump with flair,
Turns out, it's just a dog named Bear.

The trees chuckle in the soft breeze,
While ants march like they own the leaves.
I trip on roots, a ballet gone wrong,
Nature's giggles—they sing along.

A mushroom nods like an old wise sage,
It whispers secrets from yesteryear's page.
I try to listen, but I can't quite fit,
Too many laughs, I might just split!

The sun peeks through with a cheeky grin,
As shadows dance, I join in the spin.
With nature's arms, I twirl and sway,
Who needs a gym when trees want to play?

## Mosaic of Earthy Reminiscence

A patch of dirt, a canvas grand,
Where daisies paint with nature's hand.
Each flower ticks, a clock's bizarre,
Counting laughs from here to afar.

The ladybugs wear tiny hats,
While beetles waltz and chat like chaps.
Underneath a fussy old fern,
I find my lost snack—oh, that's my turn!

The breeze decides to play charades,
Tugging clothes like it's on parade.
I'm flapping like a flag so bright,
While chortling birds take mental flight.

Amongst the stones in a muddled heap,
Lie stories that giggle and silently leap.
Every rock, a memoir of old,
Whispering giggles and tales retold.

## Veils of Time in the Underbrush

In tangled paths where shadows creep,
Laughter echoes, vivid and deep.
A squirrel yells, 'Watch out below!'
While I dodge mud like a clumsy show.

A spider weaves a silly dance,
Caught in a leaf while taking a chance.
I clap my hands, it just won't quit,
That eight-legged friend, what a funny skit!

The stream bubbles with gurgles and cheer,
Replaying jokes from yesteryear.
I try to fish for wisdom, yet,
All I catch are laughs that I won't forget.

With every step, old stories bloom,
A tapestry woven in nature's room.
I smile and grin, a heart so light,
In this underbrush of sheer delight.

## Green Musings in Hidden Groves

In hidden glades where shadows twine,
Whispering leaves share tales divine.
I overhear a tree's wild jest,
About squirrels that never rest.

The grass, a carpet, tickles my toes,
While dandelions wear their bows.
I lay and laugh at clouds a-drift,
One looks like dinner—what a gift!

A bunny hops in a silly race,
Chasing memories through empty space.
Each hop a giggle, each twitch a grin,
Who knew my park was a comedy spin?

As twilight falls like a cozy quilt,
I hear the night in laughter built.
The world wraps up in a gentle sigh,
With stories of nature, oh my, oh my!

## Cradle of Nature's Footprints

In the corner of the yard so wide,
Lies a shoe that Nature can't abide.
With grass sprouting from its worn-out toe,
It tells tales of where the wild things go.

Squirrels laugh as they prance and play,
Dancing around in a cheeky display.
That forgotten sneaker, a throne for a bug,
Turns everyday strolls into a warm hug.

A frog hops by with a curious glance,
Wondrously wondering if it's a new dance.
While ants march solemnly with a big snack,
Plotting an invasion, they won't turn back.

So next time you step past the old shoe,
Remember the giggles in Nature's view.
For with every footprint, a story unfolds,
In the cradle of laughter that Nature holds.

## Nostalgia in the Underbrush

Beneath the bushes, old toys are found,
Lost in the weeds, where laughter had drowned.
A doll's head, a car, all tangled in vines,
Remind us of joy where the wild thing shines.

A rusted bike with a missing wheel,
Holds secrets of summers, it's almost surreal.
We raced with the wind, felt the sun's warm glow,
Now just a relic that time can't outgrow.

Crickets chirp tunes that echo the past,
As shadows of memories start to amass.
Each twig broke beneath childhood's spree,
A still life of laughter beneath the old tree.

So dive into laughter, let nostalgia flow,
In the underbrush, where wild winds blow.
Each corner holds whispers, each leaf hides a song,
In the tangled embrace where we once belonged.

## Veils of Life and Decay

In the garden, a grand old hat lies,
Home to a spider with eight total eyes.
It's a fashion statement of time long gone,
An outdated trend, yet still carries on.

Among wilting petals, daisies still giggle,
Tickled by breezes that make them wiggle.
Old fences sag in their rusty embrace,
While worms compose songs in their dark little space.

The sun sets low, casting shadows so long,
As crickets tune up their nightly song.
Each layer of earth holds treasures unsaid,
In the tales of the living, the fading, the dead.

So lift back the veil, see where laughter hides,
In the quirks of decay, where Nature abides.
For every turn of leaf, and rustle of clay,
Whispers of joy dance where youth used to play.

## The Stillness Between Raindrops

Between each droplet, laughter does bloom,
In puddles that shimmer, like a sapphire room.
Kids in raincoats leap, splashing on by,
As clouds above burst into bursts of shy.

A snail sets its pace, slow and unsure,
While worms throw a party in mud-covered s-lore.
Frogs wear tiny crowns, monarchs of mirth,
While daisies tiptoe, celebrating their birth.

At last, when sun peeks with a golden grin,
The world glistens bright, sparkling from within.
In the quiet that follows, there's mischief galore,
As Nature herself giggles, wanting more.

So find the humor in raindrops' retreat,
In puddles of joy where the sky and earth meet.
For in every storm, a child's laughter waits,
Defying the gloom, opening friendly gates.

## The Beauty of Forgotten Paths


Once I tripped on a tangled vine,
A squirrel laughed, said, "What a sign!"
I dusted off my prideful flares,
And marveled at the hidden layers.

Old shoes found, lost to the trees,
They fit like slippers, oh so free!
I danced with shadows, twirled with glee,
And tripped again, just to feel spree.

## In the Company of the Silent

Whispers echo in leafy coats,
While crickets strum their tiny notes.
I shared my sandwich with a bee,
As it gorged on crumbs just like me.

A ghost of laughter from the past,
High-fived a toad, not very fast!
We both agreed on this strange fate,
Plenty of time to contemplate.

## **Roots of Memory**

Beneath the bark, a tale unfolds,
Where secrets grow like marigold.
I found a shoe from '92,
And wondered why it missed the view.

The roots entwined with jaybird song,
A perfect place where I belong.
Each twist and turn, a jolly jest,
In nature's game, I'm just a guest.

## Branches of Dream

High above, the branches sway,
Squirrels plotting their next café.
They offer nuts and gossip tips,
While I'm just here, enjoying sips.

A dreamer's hat flew past a crow,
Who wore it like a fine chapeau.
We laughed until the sun went low,
What tales the tree-tops truly know!

## Shifted Stones Underfoot

Each stone I step on tells a joke,
From the pokey prickle to the oak.
They chat of shoes and lost pet plans,
While I just search for other fans.

A pebble rolled and made me yelp,
"Why chase your dreams, just sit and kelp!"
I chuckled at my wary plight,
Underneath the forest's light.

## Silvan Reveries in Twilight

In the woods where squirrels play,
A treasure map of yesterday.
I searched for coins, but found a shoe,
Guess I need a different view.

Beneath the bark, a secret dance,
Where frogs in tuxedos take a chance.
Laughter echoes, shadows tease,
Nature's stage, a playful breeze.

The mushrooms wink in subtle mirth,
A springtime giggle, Earth's rebirth.
I tell a joke, a roach laughs loud,
Such antics in the leafy crowd.

Sunsets paint the sky with glee,
While critters join the jubilee.
Twilight whispers, "Come and see,"
Where simple joys roam wild and free.

## Serene Layers of the Past

Once I tripped on roots, oh dear,
The trees all giggled, I could hear.
A snail gave me a slow salute,
While frogs applauded in their boots.

Memories wrapped in emerald wraps,
A picnic spread on old moss laps.
The ants served cake, with tiny forks,
As fireflies danced like quirky storks.

A vintage hat from '93,
Hangs on a branch, oh what glee!
It flutters down with a bow and spin,
I tip my cap, let the fun begin.

A tangle of yarn, forgotten thread,
I chased a cat, it dashed ahead.
In this green maze, loads of fun,
Each layer hides a laughing sun.

## Moss-Covered Echoes

In the glen where whispers fade,
A story told, a masquerade.
The squirrels dressed in fancy hats,
With acorns clinking, like diplomats.

A bear recounts his clumsy fall,
While mushrooms giggle, standing tall.
The sunbeams peek through leafy fans,
As shadows prance in dainty pants.

Old logs talk with creaky charm,
Each knot and groove, a lucky harm.
A snail, the poet, pens his verse,
Though every line's a little terse.

The past, a jest at nature's play,
With echoes laughing all the way.
Join in the fun, just look around,
In every nook, sweet joy's abound.

## The Green Veil of Memory


Behind the ferns, a party brews,
Where owls in pajamas share the news.
A rabbit tells of lost cabbages,
While beetles create tiny beauty pageants.

The brook puts on a splashy show,
A frog in shades says, "Come and go!"
The laughter bubbles through the glade,
As vines swing low, not one jaded shade.

In every rustle, a funny tale,
Listen close, you might turn pale.
A gnome with hiccups steals the scene,
With puns that make the flowers keen.

Under the shade, the past gives chase,
With silly memories, we embrace.
Embrace the green, let spirits rise,
In this enchanted world, where whimsy lies.

www.ingramcontent.com/pod-product-compliance
Lightning Source LLC
Chambersburg PA
CBHW071849160426
43209CB00003B/481